Ancient Greece Philosophers

E-book with AI, Volume 1

Canerk

Published by Canerk, 2023.

While every precaution has been taken in the preparation of this book, the publisher assumes no responsibility for errors or omissions, or for damages resulting from the use of the information contained herein.

ANCIENT GREECE PHILOSOPHERS

First edition. February 4, 2023.

ISBN: 979-8215827123

Written by Canerk.

Table of Contents

Ancient Greek Philosophers

The Top Twenty
Caner Kocamaz

(Philosophy For Everyone)

BOOK DESIGN BY (ANONYM)

Cover design by Anonym)
ISBN - Paperback: 123456789
ISBN - Hardcover : 123456789
First Edition: Feb 2023

Preface

Ancient Greek philosophy was a collection of ideas, theories and beliefs developed in Greece from the 6th century BCE to the 6th century CE. It covered a range of topics including ethics, metaphysics, politics, and science, and was characterized by critical thinking and questioning of traditional beliefs and conventions. The ancient Greek philosophers were known for their method of questioning and their belief in the importance of knowledge for living a virtuous life. They explored the nature of reality and the purpose of life, and many of their ideas continue to influence Western thought to this day.

1

SOCRATES

SOCRATES WAS A FAMOUS ancient Greek philosopher who lived in Athens from 470-399 BCE. He is widely considered to be the father of Western philosophy and is best known for his method of inquiry, known as the Socratic method. This method, which involves asking questions and encouraging others to think critically, is still used today in many educational settings.

Socrates was born into a working-class family in Athens and worked as a stone mason and a sculptor before turning to philosophy. Despite his humble beginnings, Socrates was known for his wisdom and was widely respected in Athens. He believed that the pursuit of knowledge was the key to a fulfilling life, and he spent much of his time walking around Athens, engaging in philosophical discussions with anyone who would listen.

One of Socrates' most famous quotes is,

"The only true wisdom is in knowing that you know nothing."

This quote speaks to his humble and curious nature, and his belief that there is always more to learn. He was also known for his self-awareness and his ability to critique his own thoughts and beliefs, as evidenced by his famous quote,

"I know that I am wise because I know that I know nothing."

Socrates was known for his questioning of conventional wisdom and his belief that people should examine their own beliefs in order to arrive at a deeper understanding of the world. He believed that people could learn more by questioning what they thought they knew than by simply accepting what they were told. This approach was revolutionary at the time, and many of Socrates' contemporaries were not happy with his questioning of the status quo.

Despite his popularity among the people of Athens, Socrates was eventually brought to trial on charges of impiety and corruption of the youth. He was sentenced to death by drinking hemlock, and his death is considered one of the greatest injustices in Western philosophy.

Socrates left no written works of his own, but his philosophy and teachings have been recorded by his students, Plato and Xenophon. These works have helped to preserve Socrates' legacy and have given us a glimpse into his thought processes and beliefs.

One of Socrates' most famous teachings is the idea of the "examined life." This idea holds that the purpose of life is to think about and understand one's beliefs, values, and actions in order to live a virtuous and fulfilling life. Socrates believed that people who do not question their beliefs and values are living an unexamined life, and that this kind of life is not worth living.

Another important aspect of Socrates' philosophy is his belief in the existence of objective truth. He believed that there is a universal standard of right and wrong that applies to all people, and that it is possible to arrive at this truth through reason and critical thinking. This belief was a cornerstone of Western philosophy and has influenced countless philosophers in the centuries since his death.

In conclusion, Socrates remains one of the most influential figures in the history of Western philosophy. His questioning of conventional wisdom, his commitment to the examined life, and his belief in objective truth have all had a lasting impact on the development of Western thought. Today, Socrates is remembered as a champion of reason and critical thinking, and his legacy continues to inspire new generations of philosophers and thinkers.

2

PLATO

PLATO WAS AN ANCIENT Greek philosopher who lived from 427/428 BC to 347/348 BC. He was a student of Socrates and a teacher of Aristotle. He was one of the most important figures in the development of Western philosophy and one of the founders of the Academy in Athens, which was one of the first institutions of higher learning in the Western world.

Plato was a prolific writer and his works have had a profound impact on Western thought and culture. His most famous works include "The Republic," "The Symposium," and "The Phaedo." In these works, Plato explored a wide range of philosophical questions, including the nature of justice, the existence of an afterlife, and the nature of reality.

One of Plato's central philosophical ideas was the theory of Forms or Ideas. According to this theory, the physical world is merely a reflection of a more perfect, eternal, and unchanging world of Forms. The Forms are the objects of true knowledge, and it is only by accessing this knowledge that one can truly understand the world.

Plato believed that the physical world is constantly changing, but the world of Forms is eternal and unchanging. This idea was central to his understanding of knowledge and truth. In his words:

"And the things that have come into being, as I was saying, have a nature relative to the perception of them, and this is called their

reality, because they are objects of perception. But the things that are always and are by nature always what they are, are in a much higher degree the objects of knowledge." (Phaedo, 75d)

Plato was also interested in the nature of morality and justice. In "The Republic," he explored the idea of a just society and the role of the philosopher-king in creating such a society. In this work, Plato argued that the pursuit of justice requires the cultivation of wisdom and virtue in both the individual and the state.

In addition to his philosophical works, Plato was also a visionary. He believed that the ideal society could only be created through the development of a new type of education. In his words:

"The first and greatest of necessities is to find a way of life for the individual which is in harmony with his own nature and that of the state...And this, my friend, is the whole aim of the present inquiry; for this is the great enterprise we have in hand." (The Republic, IV.435e)

Plato's vision of education was not just about imparting knowledge, but also about cultivating the individual's moral character. He believed that education should be a lifelong pursuit and that it was the key to creating a just and harmonious society.

In conclusion, Plato was one of the most influential figures in the development of Western philosophy. His ideas on the nature of reality, knowledge, morality, and justice continue to be studied and debated to this day. He was a visionary who believed that the pursuit of knowledge and the cultivation of virtue were essential to creating a just and harmonious society. His works remain an important part of the Western philosophical tradition and continue to inspire new generations of philosophers and thinkers.

3

Aristotle

ARISTOTLE WAS A GREEK philosopher who lived from 384 BCE to 322 BCE. He was a student of Plato and later tutored Alexander the Great. He is considered one of the greatest minds in Western philosophy and has made significant contributions in many fields, including ethics, politics, logic, and biology.

Aristotle was born in Stagira, a small town in northern Greece. His father was a physician, and Aristotle's early education was heavily influenced by his father's work, which sparked his interest in biology and the natural world. After his father's death, Aristotle traveled to Athens to study at Plato's Academy. He was an exceptional student and quickly became one of Plato's most trusted disciples.

After leaving the Academy, Aristotle spent several years traveling and conducting research. He eventually settled in Athens and founded his own school, the Lyceum, which became one of the most prestigious institutions of learning in the ancient world.

One of Aristotle's most famous works is the Nicomachean Ethics, which explores the nature of morality and the good life. Aristotle believed that the goal of human life was to achieve happiness, and that happiness could be obtained through virtuous action. He identified several virtues, including courage, justice, and temperance, and argued that a virtuous person was someone who possessed a mean between two extremes of behavior. For example, Aristotle believed that courage was the mean between cowardice and recklessness.

Another important work by Aristotle was Politics, in which he explored the nature of the state and the ideal form of government. Aristotle believed that the state was necessary for the preservation of the good life and that it was the role of the government to promote the common good. He identified several forms of government, including monarchy, aristocracy, and democracy, and argued that the best form of government was a mixed constitution, combining elements of each.

Aristotle also made significant contributions to logic and the study of argument. He developed the syllogism, a method of deductive reasoning, and his Organon contains a comprehensive treatment of the principles of reasoning and argumentation.

In addition to his philosophical work, Aristotle made important contributions to the study of biology. He conducted extensive research on the natural world and wrote extensively on zoology, botany, and physiology. He was one of the first scientists to classify living things and to develop a theory of evolution.

Aristotle's influence on Western thought cannot be overstated. His works have been studied and discussed for over 2,000 years, and his ideas continue to shape our understanding of the world.

One of Aristotle's most famous quotes is,

> *"Happiness is the meaning and the purpose of life, the whole aim and end of human existence."*

This quote speaks to Aristotle's belief that the ultimate goal of human life was to achieve happiness through virtuous action and that this was the meaning and purpose of existence.

Another famous quote by Aristotle is,

> *"The least initial deviation from the truth is multiplied later a thousandfold."*

This quote highlights Aristotle's belief in the importance of accuracy and precision in reasoning and argumentation, and how even small errors in thinking can have significant consequences later on.

In conclusion, Aristotle was a pioneering figure in Western philosophy, and his contributions to the fields of ethics, politics, logic, and biology continue to shape our understanding of the world. He was a master of reason and argument, and his works continue to be studied and discussed by philosophers, scientists, and scholars today..

4

Epicurus

EPICURUS WAS AN ANCIENT Greek philosopher born in Samos, Ionia in 341 BCE. He was a key figure in the development of Western philosophy, and his teachings have had a lasting impact on Western thought. Epicurus was a major exponent of the philosophy of Epicureanism, which aimed to promote a life of pleasure and happiness, free from pain and suffering. In this article, we will explore the life and teachings of Epicurus, and examine the impact of his philosophy on Western thought.

Epicurus was born into a well-to-do family, and he received a good education, studying under the philosopher Nausiphanes and later in Athens, where he studied under the famous philosopher Plato. After completing his education, Epicurus traveled throughout Greece, teaching and spreading his ideas. He eventually settled in Athens, where he founded a philosophical school known as The Garden. This school was dedicated to the study of philosophy, and it became a center for the study of Epicureanism.

Epicurus' philosophy centered on the idea that the ultimate goal of human life is to attain happiness and pleasure. He believed that pleasure was the highest good, and that pain and suffering should be avoided whenever possible. Epicurus believed that the way to achieve this goal was to live a life of moderation and simplicity, free from excess and extravagance. He argued that it was important to cultivate friendships and to live in peace with others, as these things would bring happiness and pleasure to our lives.

Epicurus was also a firm believer in the power of reason, and he encouraged his followers to use their minds to think critically about the world around them. He believed that it was possible to understand the natural world through observation and reason, and he taught that the universe was infinite and eternal. Epicurus was also a materialist, meaning that he believed that everything in the universe was made of matter and that there was no room for supernatural beings or forces.

One of the most famous quotes from Epicurus is,

> *"Do not waste your time on what you cannot have; think about what you can attain and make the most of it."*

This quote captures the essence of Epicurean philosophy, which emphasizes the importance of focusing on what we can control and avoiding excessive desires and fears that lead to pain and suffering.

Epicurus was also a firm believer in the importance of death, and he taught that death was nothing to be feared. He argued that death was simply the end of life, and that it was not something to be feared or mourned. Epicurus believed that the fear of death was the cause of much of the pain and suffering in the world, and that it was important to overcome this fear in order to live a happy and fulfilling life.

Epicurus' teachings had a profound impact on Western thought, and his philosophy was highly influential in ancient Greece. In the centuries following his death, Epicureanism spread throughout the Roman Empire, and his ideas were widely studied and discussed by philosophers and scholars.

Today, Epicureanism continues to be a topic of interest and study, and Epicurus' ideas continue to inspire people around the world. His teachings on the importance of moderation, simplicity, and reason remain relevant and have helped to shape the way we think about the world and our place in it.

In conclusion, Epicurus was a philosopher who made a significant contribution to Western thought. His philosophy of Epicureanism, which aimed to promote a life of pleasure and happiness, free from pain and suffering, has had a lasting impact on Western thought. Epicurus' teachings on the importance of moderation, simplicity, and reason continue to inspire people today, and his ideas continue to shape the way we think about the world and our place in.

5

Zeno of Elea

ZENO OF ELEA WAS A pre-Socratic Greek philosopher who lived in the 5th century BCE. He was born in the city of Elea, located in Southern Italy. Zeno was a student of Parmenides, who was also a philosopher from Elea and is considered one of the most important figures in the development of Western philosophy.

Zeno is best known for his paradoxes, which were a series of arguments designed to challenge the conventional understanding of space, time, and motion. These paradoxes were intended to demonstrate the limits of human reasoning and to encourage people to question their assumptions.

One of the most famous paradoxes created by Zeno is known as the Dichotomy Paradox. This paradox states that in order to reach a certain point, one must first reach halfway there. But in order to reach halfway there, one must first reach halfway to halfway there. And so on. Zeno argues that because this process goes on forever, it is impossible to reach the final destination.

Here are Zeno's words describing the Dichotomy Paradox:

"That which is in locomotion must arrive at the half-way stage before it arrives at the goal."

Another famous paradox is the Achilles and the Tortoise Paradox, which states that even if Achilles is faster than the Tortoise, he can never beat the Tortoise in a race. This paradox is based on the idea that by the time Achilles reaches the spot where the Tortoise started, the Tortoise will have moved a little further. And by the time Achilles reaches that spot, the Tortoise will have moved a little further again. Zeno argues that this process will continue forever, so it is impossible for Achilles to catch up to the Tortoise.

Zeno's words in describing this paradox are:

"In a race, the quickest runner can never overtake the slowest, since the pursuer must first reach the point whence the pursued started, so that the slower must always hold a lead."

Zeno's paradoxes were influential in shaping the course of Western philosophy. They helped to lay the foundations for the development of logic and critical thinking. Additionally, his ideas about space and time inspired later philosophers, such as Plato and Aristotle, to think more deeply about these concepts and to develop their own theories about them.

In conclusion, Zeno of Elea was a pre-Socratic Greek philosopher who was born in the 5th century BCE in the city of Elea. He was a student of Parmenides and is best known for his paradoxes, which challenged the conventional understanding of space, time, and motion.

These paradoxes were intended to demonstrate the limits of human reasoning and to encourage people to question their assumptions. Zeno's ideas continue to be studied and discussed by philosophers, and his paradoxes remain relevant to this day.

6

Pythagoras

PYTHAGORAS WAS AN ANCIENT Greek philosopher who lived from around 570 BCE to 495 BCE. He is widely considered to be one of the most influential figures in the development of Western mathematics and philosophy. Born on the island of Samos, Pythagoras moved to Croton, Italy where he founded the Pythagorean Brotherhood, a community of individuals devoted to the pursuit of knowledge and wisdom.

Pythagoras was a multifaceted individual with a wide range of interests and skills. He was known for his mathematical theories, which formed the basis for the development of modern mathematics. His most famous theorem, the Pythagorean theorem, states that in a right-angled triangle, the square of the length of the hypotenuse (the side opposite the right angle) is equal to the sum of the squares of the lengths of the other two sides. This theorem has been used for centuries in the fields of mathematics, engineering, and science, and is still widely taught in schools today.

In addition to his mathematical theories, Pythagoras was also known for his philosophical beliefs. He believed in the concept of the transmigration of souls, which holds that the soul of a person is reborn into another body after death. He also believed in the existence of a divine, spiritual realm and the importance of living a virtuous life in order to achieve a harmonious existence in both this life and the next.

Pythagoras was a firm believer in the power of mathematics and its role in understanding the universe. He believed that everything in the world could be reduced to numbers and that the relationships between numbers held the key to understanding the mysteries of the universe. He once said,

"Number is the ruler of forms and ideas, and the cause of gods and demons."

Pythagoras was also a passionate advocate for the importance of a healthy and balanced lifestyle. He encouraged his followers to live a life of simplicity, abstaining from material possessions and focusing instead on spiritual growth and intellectual pursuits. He believed that a life of excess, whether it be in terms of food, drink, or other material possessions, would only lead to disharmony and suffering.

One of the most interesting aspects of Pythagoras's life and work was his emphasis on the power of music. He believed that music had the ability to heal the soul and that the harmonious relationships between musical notes could be used to understand the harmonious relationships between all things in the universe. He famously said,

"There is geometry in the humming of the strings, there is music in the spacing of the spheres."

Despite the significant impact that Pythagoras had on the development of mathematics and philosophy, very little is known about his life and work. Many of the stories and beliefs associated with him were passed down through the generations by his followers and it is difficult to separate fact from fiction. Nevertheless, the legacy of Pythagoras lives on and his influence can still be seen in a wide range of fields, including mathematics, philosophy, and music.

In conclusion, Pythagoras was a remarkable individual who made a significant contribution to the development of Western mathematics and philosophy. His ideas and beliefs continue to inspire and influence people to this day. He was a firm believer in the power of mathematics, the importance of living a virtuous life, and the role of music in understanding the universe. His ideas and beliefs continue to inspire people to this day and his legacy will be remembered for generations to come.

7

Anaxagoras

ANAXAGORAS WAS A PRE-Socratic Greek philosopher who lived in the 5th century BCE. He was born in Clazomenae, an Ionian city, and was one of the first natural philosophers to introduce the idea of an infinite universe and the concept of Nous, or Mind.

Anaxagoras was a student of Anaximenes, and he later travelled to Athens, where he became a friend of Pericles. He taught philosophy in Athens for 30 years and was known for his unorthodox ideas and his love of science and knowledge.

ONE OF ANAXAGORAS'S most famous quotes is,

"All things were together, infinite both in number and in smallness."

This quote highlights his belief that the universe is made up of an infinite number of small particles, which he referred to as "seeds." These seeds were the building blocks of all matter and were responsible for the creation of the world.

Anaxagoras was also known for his belief that the Sun and the Moon were rocks, and that they were not gods as was commonly believed at the time. He believed that the Sun was a hot rock, while the Moon was a cold one. This was a radical idea at the time and led to his indictment for impiety by the Athenian government. However, he was acquitted after a trial, and he continued to teach and write about his ideas.

Another famous quote by Anaxagoras is,

"There is a portion of everything in everything."

This quote highlights his belief that everything in the universe contains a small portion of everything else. He believed that everything was made up of a mixture of the seeds, and that the different properties of things were due to the different proportions of seeds they contained.

Anaxagoras was also known for his idea that Nous, or Mind, was responsible for the order and organization of the universe. He believed that Nous was the cause of all things and that it was the source of all knowledge and wisdom. This idea was a major contribution to the development of philosophy and the idea of a guiding principle in the universe.

In addition to his philosophical beliefs, Anaxagoras was also known for his scientific pursuits. He was one of the first people to study meteorology and he made important contributions to our understanding of the natural world. He also believed that the stars were other suns and that there were other worlds like our own.

Anaxagoras's ideas were a major influence on later philosophers, including Socrates, Plato, and Aristotle. He was also an important figure in the development of science and the study of the natural world.

In conclusion, Anaxagoras was a pioneer of natural philosophy and a major contributor to our understanding of the universe. His ideas on the infinite universe, the idea of Nous, and his scientific pursuits were groundbreaking and had a lasting impact on the development of philosophy and science. His love of knowledge and his unorthodox ideas continue to inspire and captivate people to this day.

8

Democritus

DEMOCRITUS WAS A GREEK philosopher who lived in the 5th century BCE. He was born in Abdera, Thrace and was a contemporary of Socrates. He is best known for his atomic theory, which posits that matter is composed of indivisible particles known as atoms. This theory was a radical departure from the prevailing view in ancient Greece, which held that matter was continuous and indivisible.

Democritus was a student of Leucippus, another philosopher who is credited with developing the atomic theory. Together, they were known as the Atomists. Democritus wrote extensively on the nature of reality and matter, and his works covered a wide range of topics, including ethics, metaphysics, and epistemology.

One of the most famous quotes of Democritus is:

"By convention sweet, by convention bitter, by convention hot, by convention cold, by convention color; but in reality atoms and void."

This quote highlights Democritus's belief that our perception of reality is shaped by our experiences and cultural conventions, rather than by the objective nature of reality.

Democritus was also known for his ethical views. He believed that happiness was the ultimate goal of human life, and that it could be achieved through wisdom and the avoidance of pleasure. He held that pleasure was fleeting and did not provide lasting happiness, and that wisdom was the key to a virtuous life.

Another famous quote of Democritus is:

"The wise man does not grieve for the things he has not, but rejoices for those which he has."

This quote highlights Democritus's belief in the importance of finding happiness in one's present circumstances, rather than being overly focused on what one lacks.

Democritus was also interested in the nature of knowledge. He believed that knowledge was based on sense perception, and that the mind was able to form accurate representations of reality through the senses. He held that the senses were reliable, but that some of our beliefs could be false due to the limitations of the senses and the influence of cultural and personal biases.

Democritus's atomic theory was a significant contribution to the development of science and philosophy. It laid the foundation for the development of modern atomic theory and influenced later philosophers, such as Epicurus, who developed his own atomic theory based on Democritus's work.

In conclusion, Democritus was a versatile and influential philosopher who made significant contributions to our understanding of the nature of reality, matter, and ethics. His atomic theory challenged prevailing views in ancient Greece and laid the foundation for the development of modern atomic theory. His quotes continue to be relevant today, and his views on the nature of reality, pleasure, and wisdom are as relevant now as they were in ancient Greece.

9

Heraclitus of Ephesus

HERACLITUS OF EPHESUS, born around 535 BCE, was an ancient Greek philosopher who is best known for his doctrine of change being central to the universe. He was called "The Obscure" due to the enigmatic and paradoxical nature of his sayings, which were recorded by later ancient commentators. Despite the lack of comprehensive written works by Heraclitus, his philosophy has had a lasting impact on Western thought, influencing the likes of Plato, Aristotle, and later thinkers like Nietzsche and Heidegger.

Heraclitus believed that the universe was in a constant state of flux and change, a concept he famously encapsulated in his saying,

"You cannot step into the same river twice".

He argued that everything is in a state of becoming and that change is the only constant. This idea was in stark contrast to the prevailing view in ancient Greece, which held that the universe was unchanging and eternal. Heraclitus saw the world as being governed by logos, or reason, which he believed was the underlying order of the universe. This idea of logos also had a moral dimension, as Heraclitus believed that individuals who lived in accordance with the logos would live a virtuous life.

One of Heraclitus's most famous sayings is,

"The world is an ever-living fire, kindled in measures and extinguished in measures".

This metaphor was used to express his belief that the universe was in a constant state of change, with things being born and dying, and that the process of change was governed by logos. Heraclitus saw this process as being cyclical, with the same things being born and dying over and over again, in a never-ending cycle.

Heraclitus was also known for his critiques of conventional wisdom and societal norms. He famously said,

"The majority of people are as unaware of their own ignorance as they are of their own wisdom".

This statement reflects his belief that people often blindly accept conventional wisdom and do not question the beliefs and values that are handed down to them. Heraclitus saw the pursuit of wisdom as being an individual journey, and he believed that people should strive to understand the world for themselves, rather than simply accepting the opinions of others.

Another famous saying of Heraclitus is,

"War is the father of all things".

This statement was intended to convey the idea that conflict and struggle are central to the universe and that they drive change and development. Heraclitus believed that conflict was necessary for progress and growth, and that without it, the world would stagnate. He saw conflict as being a part of the natural cycle of change, and he believed that it was essential for the world to continue to evolve.

Heraclitus was also known for his skepticism of the gods and religion. He famously said,

"The gods are the same to all people, but the wise understand them in a different way".

This statement reflected his belief that people often misunderstand the gods and their role in the world. Heraclitus saw the gods as being a part of the natural world, rather than being separate and distinct from it. He believed that people should strive to understand the gods as they are, rather than accepting popular misconceptions about them.

In conclusion, Heraclitus was a seminal figure in ancient Greek philosophy whose ideas have had a lasting impact on Western thought. Despite the lack of comprehensive written works by Heraclitus, his sayings have been passed down through the centuries and continue to be studied and debated by philosophers and scholars. His doctrine of change being central to the universe, his critiques of conventional wisdom and societal norms, and his belief in the importance of individual understanding, have all had a profound.

10

Parmenides

PARMENIDES WAS A PRE-Socratic Greek philosopher who lived in the 5th century BCE and was born in Elea, a city in southern Italy. He is considered one of the most significant figures in Western philosophy, and his work had a profound impact on the development of Western thought. Parmenides was a monist, meaning he believed that there was only one ultimate reality, and that all apparent differences in the world were mere illusions.

Parmenides' philosophy was rooted in the idea of the unity and unchanging nature of reality. He believed that all things in the world were eternal and unchanging, and that there was no such thing as motion, change, or coming into being. This was in direct opposition to the views of the other pre-Socratic philosophers, who believed that the world was in constant flux, and that everything was constantly changing. Parmenides believed that reality was a single, unchanging entity that was beyond space, time, and matter.

One of the most famous quotes from Parmenides is,

"What is, is, and what is not, is not."

This quote captures the essence of his philosophy and is often considered a foundational principle of Western philosophy. Parmenides believed that all things in the world were either real or not real, and that there was no middle ground between these two states.

Another important aspect of Parmenides' philosophy was his belief in the distinction between appearance and reality. He believed that what we see in the world around us is not a true reflection of reality, but rather a mere appearance that is shaped by our perceptions and beliefs. He argued that the senses are deceptive, and that true knowledge can only be gained through reason and logic.

Parmenides also made significant contributions to the field of logic and metaphysics. He was one of the first philosophers to argue that a thing could not both be and not be at the same time, a principle that would later be known as the law of non-contradiction. He also believed that all things in the world were interconnected and that the universe was a single, harmonious entity.

In his poem "On Nature," Parmenides lays out his philosophy in detail. The poem is written in the form of a dialogue between the poet and a goddess who leads him on a journey of discovery. In the poem, the goddess explains to the poet that there are two paths of inquiry: the path of truth and the path of deception. She tells the poet that the path of truth leads to a proper understanding of reality, while the path of deception leads to error and ignorance.

One of the most famous quotes from Parmenides' poem is,

> *"The only way of inquiry that can be thought of is that it is, and that it is not possible not to be."*

This quote captures the essence of Parmenides' belief in the unity and unchanging nature of reality. He believed that all things in the world were real and could not not be, and that there was no such thing as non-being.

Parmenides' philosophy had a profound impact on later philosophers, particularly the great philosophers of the Western tradition such as Plato and Aristotle. His ideas about the unity and unchanging nature of reality, the distinction between appearance and reality, and the importance of reason and logic continue to be studied and discussed today.

In conclusion, Parmenides was a pioneering figure in the development of Western philosophy. His ideas about the unity and unchanging nature of reality, the distinction between appearance and reality, and the importance of reason and logic continue to be relevant and influential even today. His poetry and prose remain a testament to his philosophical genius and the lasting impact of his ideas on Western thought.

11

Thales of Miletus

THALES OF MILETUS WAS an ancient Greek philosopher and one of the Seven Sages of Greece, who lived around the mid-6th century BC. He was born in Miletus, a city located on the western coast of modern-day Turkey and is considered to be one of the earliest Greek philosophers and mathematicians.

Thales was known for his wisdom and his practical, down-to-earth approach to philosophy. He believed in the power of reason and observation and sought to understand the natural world through observation and experimentation. He was also one of the first people to propose a natural explanation for the phenomenon of the world, rather than attributing it to the gods.

One of Thales' most famous quotes is,

"Know thyself,"

which he inscribed on the temple at Delphi. This phrase is often interpreted as a call to self-reflection and self-awareness and is considered to be a cornerstone of ancient Greek philosophy. Thales also believed that wisdom was the most important aspect of life, and that the pursuit of knowledge should be the ultimate goal of humanity.

Thales is also known for his contributions to mathematics and geometry. He is said to have discovered the theorem that the base angles of an isosceles triangle are equal, and he was also the first person to use geometry for practical purposes, such as surveying land and determining the height of buildings and pyramids.

Thales was also a political and economic thinker and was known for his business acumen. He was said to have made a fortune by predicting a bumper olive crop and buying up all the olive presses before the harvest, allowing him to control the market and charge high prices for the oil. This story is often used as an example of his clever and innovative thinking, and his ability to see opportunities where others saw only difficulties.

Despite his many accomplishments, Thales was also a humble man, who never sought to draw attention to himself or his achievements. He was known for his simplicity and his modest lifestyle, and lived a life of simplicity and asceticism, focusing on his studies and his search for knowledge.

In conclusion, Thales of Miletus was a remarkable figure who had a profound impact on the ancient world. He was a pioneering philosopher and mathematician, who used his powers of observation and reason to understand the natural world and the workings of the universe. His wisdom and practical approach to life have made him a timeless figure who continues to inspire and influence people to this day.

One of Thales' famous quotes,

"The most difficult thing in life is to know yourself,"

speaks to the importance of self-reflection and self-awareness, and serves as a reminder of the timeless wisdom that Thales has left behind.

12

Anaximander

ANAXIMANDER WAS A PRE-Socratic Greek philosopher who lived in the 6th century BCE. He was a student of Thales and is considered to be one of the earliest philosophers in the Western tradition. Anaximander was born in Miletus, an ancient city located on the coast of Asia Minor (modern-day Turkey).

Anaximander was known for his contributions to several areas of thought, including astronomy, geography, and philosophy. He is considered to be one of the first thinkers to attempt to explain the natural world in terms of natural causes, rather than attributing events to the actions of the gods.

One of Anaximander's most famous ideas was his theory of the origin of the universe. According to Anaximander, the universe was originally an infinite, undifferentiated mass known as the "apeiron". This mass was eternal and self-generating, and it gave birth to everything that exists in the world today.

Anaximander believed that the earth was a cylinder-shaped body floating in the universe, and he was the first person to create a map of the known world. He also made contributions to astronomy, as he believed that the stars were attached to a celestial sphere and that the moon was illuminated by the sun.

Anaximander was also a philosopher who was interested in ethics and morality. He believed that justice was a cosmic principle that governed the universe, and that human beings should strive to live in harmony with this principle. He believed that the universe was governed by laws, and that the ultimate goal of human life was to understand these laws and live in accordance with them.

One of Anaximander's famous quotes is,

"The first principle is the infinite, and it is indeterminate, for they say it is neither water nor any other of the so-called elements, but some other nature which is unlimited."

This quote expresses his belief in the existence of an eternal, undifferentiated principle that gave birth to everything that exists in the world.

Another famous quote of Anaximander is,

"The origin of things is the infinite, and the end of things is the infinite."

This quote expresses his belief that the universe has no beginning or end, and that everything is part of an eternal cycle of creation and destruction.

In conclusion, Anaximander was a groundbreaking philosopher who made significant contributions to several areas of thought. He was one of the first thinkers to attempt to explain the natural world in terms of natural causes, and his ideas about the origin of the universe, ethics, and morality had a lasting impact on the Western philosophical tradition. Despite the limited number of his writings that have survived to the present day, his ideas continue to influence contemporary thought and provide a valuable perspective on the early development of Western philosophy.

13

Leucippus

LEUCIPPUS WAS AN ANCIENT Greek philosopher who lived in the 5th century BCE and was one of the earliest proponents of atomism, a theory that the universe was composed of indivisible, indestructible particles called atoms. He is also considered to be one of the first philosophers of the Western world.

Although very little is known about Leucippus's life, he is believed to have been born in Miletus, an ancient Greek city in Asia Minor, and to have studied under the philosopher Anaximenes. Some sources also claim that he was a student of Parmenides, another important early philosopher.

Leucippus's philosophy was focused on the nature of reality, and he believed that the world was made up of tiny, imperceptible particles that could not be seen or divided further. These particles, he believed, were in constant motion and were responsible for the creation and destruction of all matter. He believed that this atomic theory provided a more accurate explanation of reality than the earlier theories of the Milesian philosophers, who believed that the world was made up of a single substance, such as air or water.

In addition to his atomism, Leucippus is also credited with the development of the concept of the void, which he believed was the space between atoms. He argued that the void was not a form of emptiness, but rather a real, physical entity that was essential to the existence of matter.

According to Leucippus, atoms would not be able to move and change without the void, and the void would not exist without the atoms.

One of Leucippus's most famous quotes is,

"Nothing can come from nothing."

This statement reflects his belief that matter could not be created or destroyed but could only change form. He believed that everything in the world, including the atoms themselves, had always existed and would always exist, and that the world was in a constant state of change.

Leucippus's ideas were further developed and expanded upon by his student and collaborator, Democritus. Together, they are considered to be the founders of atomism, and their ideas had a significant impact on the development of Western philosophy. Atomism influenced later philosophers such as Epicurus, who built upon their ideas to create his own philosophy of epicureanism.

In conclusion, Leucippus was an important early philosopher who is best known for his theory of atomism and the concept of the void. Despite the limited information that remains about his life and works, his ideas had a lasting impact on the development of Western philosophy and science, and continue to be studied and discussed by philosophers and scientists today.

Some of Leucippus's other quotes include:

"The whole is greater than the sum of its parts."

"There are things which are known, and things which are unknown, and in between are doors."

"Atoms are invisible, but their effects are visible."

14

Xenophon

XENOPHON WAS A PROMINENT ancient Greek philosopher and historian who lived between 430-354 BCE. He was a disciple of Socrates and was known for his contributions to philosophy and history. He was born in Athens and was part of the Socratic school of thought. He was also a soldier, an athlete, and a wealthy landowner.

Xenophon's philosophy was largely shaped by his association with Socrates and his belief in living a virtuous life. He believed that wisdom and virtue were closely related, and that a person's ultimate goal should be to live a life of moral and ethical excellence. In his book "Memorabilia," Xenophon provides insight into the teachings of Socrates, describing him as a man who taught people to live virtuous lives and to seek wisdom through questioning and self-reflection.

One of Xenophon's most famous quotes is,

> *"The bravest are surely those who have the clearest vision of what is before them, glory and danger alike, and yet notwithstanding, go out to meet it."*

This quote highlights Xenophon's belief in the importance of courage and bravery in the face of adversity. He believed that people should face their fears and confront challenges head-on, in order to achieve greatness and live fulfilling lives.

In addition to his philosophical contributions, Xenophon was also a historian who wrote several historical works. One of his most famous works is "Anabasis," which is a history of the failed expedition of the 10,000 Greek soldiers who were hired to fight for the Persian prince Cyrus the Younger. The work provides a vivid description of the struggles and hardships faced by the soldiers, and it also provides insight into the political and military landscape of ancient Greece and Persia.

Another notable work by Xenophon is "The Education of Cyrus," which provides a comprehensive look at the life and reign of Cyrus the Great, the founder of the Persian Empire. Xenophon portrays Cyrus as a wise and just ruler who was dedicated to promoting peace and prosperity throughout his kingdom. This work highlights Xenophon's belief in the importance of good leadership and provides valuable lessons for those seeking to lead just and effective lives.

In conclusion, Xenophon was a highly influential ancient Greek philosopher and historian who made significant contributions to both philosophy and history. He was a disciple of Socrates and was known for his belief in living a virtuous life and seeking wisdom through self-reflection and questioning. His works, including "Memorabilia," "Anabasis," and "The Education of Cyrus," provide valuable insights into the teachings of Socrates and the political and military landscape of ancient Greece and Persia. Xenophon's legacy continues to inspire people to this day, as his writings provide a window into the ancient world and offer timeless lessons for living a virtuous and fulfilling life

15

Diogenes of Sinope

Diogenes of Sinope was an ancient Greek philosopher who lived in the 4th century BCE. He was a prominent figure in the development of Cynicism, a philosophical movement that emphasized living a simple and virtuous life, free from material desires and social conventions. Diogenes was known for his unconventional lifestyle and bold statements, which challenged the values of his time. He is remembered today as a symbol of anti-establishment and individualism.

Diogenes was born in the Greek colony of Sinope in present-day Turkey. Little is known about his early life, but he is said to have lived a lavish lifestyle until he was exiled for counterfeiting money. After his exile, Diogenes lived a life of poverty and wandering, seeking wisdom and truth. He eventually settled in Athens, where he became a well-known figure for his unconventional behavior and confrontational attitude towards social norms.

Diogenes lived in a tub, slept in the open air, and ate only what was necessary to sustain himself. He rejected wealth, fame, and power, and instead lived a life of simplicity and self-sufficiency. He is famously quoted as saying,

"I have nothing, but I have everything."

This rejection of material possessions and societal conventions earned him the title of "The Dog" (from the Greek word "kuon" which means dog), and his followers became known as Cynics.

Diogenes was not only known for his unconventional lifestyle but also for his bold statements and confrontational attitude. He once offered Alexander the Great a chance to stand out of his sun, claiming that he was blocking it. He was also known for his wit and sarcasm, famously quipping,

"I am a citizen of the world."

This statement reflected his belief that all people are equal, regardless of their social status or nationality.

Diogenes also had strong views on morality and ethics. He believed that virtue was the only true wealth and that people should live honest and truthful lives, free from the influence of wealth and power. He once said,

> *"It is not that I am mad, it is only that my mind has been clarified."*

This reflected his belief that living a virtuous life, free from material desires, brought clarity and wisdom.

In addition to his beliefs about morality and ethics, Diogenes was also known for his teachings about the nature of man. He believed that people were naturally social animals, and that society corrupted them. He said, "Man is the most intelligent of the animals – and the most silly." This statement reflected his belief that people were capable of great wisdom and intelligence, but were often held back by their foolish and misguided beliefs and desires.

Diogenes of Sinope's teachings and unconventional lifestyle have made him a symbol of anti-establishment and individualism. His rejection of material possessions and social norms has inspired countless people over the centuries to question the status quo and live lives of their own choosing. His bold statements and confrontational attitude continue to challenge people to think critically about their beliefs and values.

In conclusion, Diogenes of Sinope was a pioneering figure in the development of Cynicism and a symbol of anti-establishment and individualism. His rejection of material possessions, societal norms, and his bold statements continue to inspire people to question their beliefs and values and live lives of their own choosing. His teachings about morality, ethics, and the nature of man, combined with his unconventional lifestyle, have cemented his place in history as one of the most influential philosophers of all time..

.

16

Epictetus

EPICTETUS WAS A GREEK philosopher who lived from 55 AD to 135 AD. He was born as a slave but went on to become one of the most influential thinkers of his time. He was a Stoic philosopher, and his teachings emphasized the importance of personal responsibility and the ability to control one's own thoughts and emotions.

Epictetus believed that the key to a happy and fulfilling life was to focus on things that are within our control and to accept the things that are outside of our control. He taught that it is not events themselves that cause us suffering, but rather our thoughts and reactions to those events. He encouraged his followers to adopt a detached and rational perspective, and to cultivate a strong inner self that is immune to external events.

One of the most famous quotes from Epictetus is, "

> *It's not what happens to you, but how you react to it that matters."*

This quote captures the essence of his philosophy and highlights the importance of taking control of one's own thoughts and emotions. Epictetus taught that the only things in life that we truly have control over are our own thoughts and actions, and that we should strive to cultivate a peaceful and contented state of mind, regardless of the circumstances we find ourselves in.

Another famous quote from Epictetus is,

"Don't explain your philosophy. Embody it."

This quote emphasizes the importance of living one's beliefs, rather than simply talking about them. According to Epictetus, the true test of a philosophy is whether it leads to a happy and fulfilling life, and he believed that this could only be achieved through consistent action and lived experience.

Epictetus also taught that we should be mindful of our thoughts and actions, and that we should strive to live in accordance with our values and beliefs. He encouraged his followers to cultivate a strong sense of self-awareness, and to be mindful of their thoughts and emotions, so that they could better control their reactions to external events.

Epictetus believed that happiness and contentment are the ultimate goals of life, and that these could only be achieved through the practice of philosophy. He encouraged his followers to adopt a Stoic philosophy of life, and to focus on developing a strong inner self that is immune to the ups and downs of external events.

In conclusion, Epictetus was a Greek philosopher who lived in the first and second centuries AD. He was a Stoic philosopher who emphasized the importance of personal responsibility and the ability to control one's own thoughts and emotions. He encouraged his followers to cultivate a detached and rational perspective, and to focus on things that are within their control. His teachings continue to be widely read and studied to this day, and his quotes remain as relevant and powerful as ever.

17

Hippocrates

HIPPOCRATES WAS AN ancient Greek physician, who lived between 460-370 BCE and was considered one of the most important figures in the history of medicine. He was born on the island of Kos, in the Aegean Sea, and is known as the father of modern medicine. Hippocrates was a prolific writer and his work, which includes over 70 texts, is considered a cornerstone of Western medical thought.

Hippocrates believed that health was not just the absence of disease, but a harmonious balance of the physical, mental, and spiritual aspects of life. He emphasized the importance of a healthy lifestyle and diet, and believed that the natural processes of the body could cure many illnesses. He also believed in the importance of observation and examination in diagnosing and treating patients.

One of the most famous quotes of Hippocrates is

"Let food be thy medicine and medicine be thy food."

This quote highlights his belief that a healthy diet is essential for good health. He believed that a diet should be balanced and tailored to the individual's needs and that the type of food consumed could have a significant impact on a person's health. He emphasized the importance of fresh, whole foods and discouraged the consumption of processed and refined foods.

Another famous quote by Hippocrates is

"Natural forces within us are the true healers of disease."

This quote reflects his belief in the body's natural ability to heal itself and that the role of the physician was to support and facilitate this process. He believed that the body has its own innate wisdom and that, when given the right conditions, it could heal itself. He emphasized the importance of a holistic approach to medicine, recognizing the interconnectedness of the body, mind, and spirit.

Hippocrates also believed in the importance of mental and emotional health and the impact that these factors could have on physical health. He wrote extensively about the role of stress and negative emotions in causing and exacerbating illness. He believed that a calm and peaceful state of mind was essential for good health and recommended practices such as meditation and mindfulness to promote mental and emotional well-being.

One of his famous quotes on mental and emotional health is "

Walking is man's best medicine."

This quote highlights the importance of physical activity in maintaining good health and well-being. He believed that regular exercise was essential for both physical and mental health and that it could be used to treat and prevent many illnesses.

Hippocrates also made significant contributions to the field of ethics in medicine. He believed that the physician's primary duty was to the patient and that the physician's actions should always be guided by a commitment to the patient's well-being. He wrote extensively about the importance of informed consent and the physician's duty to respect the patient's autonomy.

One of his famous quotes on medical ethics is

"First, do no harm."

This quote is now widely used in the medical profession and serves as a reminder of the physician's ethical duty to prioritize the patient's safety and well-being.

In conclusion, Hippocrates was a visionary and trailblazer in the field of medicine. His ideas and teachings continue to influence modern medicine and are still relevant today. His focus on a holistic approach to health, the importance of a healthy lifestyle and diet, and the recognition of the interplay between the physical, mental, and emotional aspects of health have all had a lasting impact on the field of medicine.

18

Empedocles

EMPEDOCLES WAS AN ANCIENT Greek philosopher and poet who lived in the 5th century BCE. He was born in Acragas, Sicily and is considered to be one of the last great presocratic philosophers. Empedocles was known for his philosophical views on the natural world, his belief in the four elements and his concept of the love and strife forces. He was also a major figure in the development of the idea of reincarnation.

Empedocles believed that the universe was made up of four elements - earth, air, fire, and water - which were in a constant state of change and mixture. He believed that these elements were eternally in flux, coming together and breaking apart in different combinations to form the world as we know it. Empedocles saw these elements as the basic building blocks of matter, and he believed that the combination of these elements could account for all physical phenomena.

Empedocles also believed in the existence of two cosmic forces, which he called "love" and "strife." According to Empedocles, love was the force that held the universe together, causing the elements to mix and come together in harmonious combinations. Strife, on the other hand, was the force that drove the elements apart, causing them to break apart into their constituent parts. Empedocles saw these two forces as being in a constant struggle with each other, with love and strife each alternately gaining the upper hand.

Empedocles believed that the physical world was not the only realm of existence. He believed that the soul was immortal and that it was reincarnated after death. According to Empedocles, the soul was a mixture of the four elements and it could be reincarnated into different forms, such as plants or animals, based on its deeds in previous lives.

Empedocles was also known for his religious views and his belief in the existence of gods. He believed that the gods were immortal beings who were the causes of natural events, such as earthquakes and thunderstorms. Empedocles saw the gods as being beyond human understanding, and he believed that they could not be known through reason or observation.

One of the most famous quotes attributed to Empedocles is,

"Man is a polyp of many forms."

This quote reflects Empedocles' belief in reincarnation, as he saw the soul as being capable of taking on many different forms in its journey through the cycles of birth and death. Another famous quote from Empedocles is,

"All things are born from earth and water, but air and fire are controlling powers."

THIS QUOTE HIGHLIGHTS Empedocles' belief in the four elements and their role in shaping the physical world.

In conclusion, Empedocles was a complex and influential philosopher whose ideas about the natural world, the forces of love and strife, and the nature of the soul have had a lasting impact on Western thought. Despite the many centuries that have passed since his death, his teachings continue to be studied and debated by scholars and students of philosophy. Empedocles' legacy is a testament to the enduring power of his ideas and the lasting impact that they have had on the development of Western thought.

19

Plotinus

PLOTINUS WAS A GREEK philosopher who lived in the Roman Empire in the 3rd century AD. He was the founder of Neoplatonism, a philosophical system that combined elements of Platonic philosophy with ideas from the mysticism of the East. Plotinus' philosophy aimed to achieve a union with the divine through contemplation and the use of reason.

Plotinus was born in Egypt, and he studied in Alexandria, which was a center of learning in the ancient world. After traveling to various parts of the Mediterranean and learning from various philosophers, he settled in Rome where he established a school of philosophy. He wrote numerous treatises on philosophy, including the Enneads, a collection of 54 essays that discussed topics such as the nature of the soul, the universe, and the divine.

One of Plotinus' key ideas was that the universe was hierarchical, with the highest level being the One, or the divine principle. He believed that the One was the source of all reality, and that everything else in the universe was a reflection of this divine principle. He wrote,

"The One is beyond being, and yet it is the source of all being."

Plotinus also believed in the existence of the soul, which he saw as a reflection of the divine principle. He believed that the soul could achieve union with the divine through contemplation and the use of reason. He wrote,

> *"The soul is a shining light, and when it is purified, it becomes one with the divine."*

In addition to his beliefs about the soul, Plotinus also had a strong view on ethics. He believed that the purpose of human life was to achieve union with the divine, and that this could be accomplished through virtuous living and the practice of philosophy. He wrote,

> *"The path to the divine is through virtue, and the practice of philosophy is the path to virtue."*

Plotinus' philosophy had a profound influence on later philosophers, particularly in the Christian and Islamic worlds. His ideas on the hierarchical structure of the universe and the importance of contemplation and reason were highly influential in the development of medieval Christian philosophy.

His ideas on ethics and the importance of virtuous living also had an impact on later thinkers, including Saint Augustine, who was heavily influenced by Plotinus' ideas when he developed his own philosophy. Plotinus' ideas on the soul and the divine were also an important influence on later Islamic philosophy, particularly in the work of the philosopher al-Farabi.

Overall, Plotinus' philosophy continues to be studied and debated by philosophers today, and his ideas continue to have a profound impact on our understanding of the universe and our place in it. He remains one of the most important figures in the history of philosophy, and his ideas continue to inspire and influence philosophers and thinkers to this day.

In conclusion, Plotinus was a philosopher who aimed to achieve union with the divine through contemplation and the use of reason. His ideas on the hierarchical structure of the universe, the soul, and ethics had a profound influence on later philosophers and continue to be studied and debated to this day.

20

Proclus

PROCLUS, ALSO KNOWN as Proclus Diadochus, was a Greek philosopher who lived in the 5th century CE and was considered one of the last great Neoplatonists. He was born in Constantinople and lived and taught in Athens, where he was known as one of the leading philosophers of his time. Proclus was highly respected and influential, both during his lifetime and in the centuries that followed.

Proclus was a profound thinker, known for his vast knowledge and understanding of the works of his predecessors, particularly those of Plato and Aristotle. He studied and taught mathematics, astronomy, and theology, and his work focused on the philosophy of Neoplatonism, which sought to reconcile the ideas of Plato and Aristotle. Proclus believed in the existence of a single, ultimate reality, which he called the One, and that all things in the universe were derived from this ultimate reality.

One of Proclus's most famous quotes is,

> *"Theology is the science which treats of the nature of the gods and their government of the world."*

This quote highlights Proclus's belief in the importance of understanding the nature of the divine and the role it plays in governing the universe. He saw theology as a fundamental aspect of philosophy and believed that understanding the gods and their relationship to the world was essential to understanding the nature of reality itself.

Proclus was also a prolific writer, leaving behind a wealth of works on various subjects, including mathematics, astronomy, and philosophy. His works include "A Commentary on the First Book of Euclid's Elements", "A Commentary on the Timaeus of Plato", and "The Elements of Theology". In these works, Proclus drew on the ideas of Plato and Aristotle, as well as his own unique insights, to develop a comprehensive system of thought.

Proclus's philosophy had a profound impact on the development of Western thought, and his ideas have been studied and debated for centuries. In particular, his ideas about the nature of reality and the role of the divine have been highly influential in the development of Western philosophy and theology.

Another famous quote of Proclus is,

"We must see things not only with the eyes but with the mind."

This quote highlights Proclus's belief in the importance of understanding reality through both observation and contemplation. He believed that it was essential to use both reason and intuition to truly understand the world around us.

Proclus was a highly revered philosopher in his own time, and his influence has been felt for centuries. His works continue to be widely studied and admired, and his ideas have had a lasting impact on the development of Western philosophy and theology.

In conclusion, Proclus was a Greek philosopher of great insight and knowledge, who lived in the 5th century CE. He was known for his vast knowledge and understanding of the works of his predecessors, and for his contribution to the philosophy of Neoplatonism. Proclus believed in the existence of a single, ultimate reality, which he called the One, and that all things in the universe were derived from this ultimate reality. He saw theology as a fundamental aspect of philosophy and believed that understanding the gods and their relationship to the world was essential to understanding the nature of reality itself. Proclus's ideas have had a lasting impact on Western thought, and his works continue to be widely studied and admired.

About the Author

The author has long been interested in ancient Greek philosophy. This book consists of information gathered by an artificial intelligence application.

www.linkedin.com/in/caner-k-75092112a/

Acknowledgement

I am truly grateful for Chatgpt's assistance. It's kindness and expertise are greatly appreciated.

About the Author

Caner Kocamaz is a dedicated follower of philosophy, with a particular interest in Ancient Greek philosophy. Born and raised in Turkey, Caner's passion for the subject began during his undergraduate studies in literature, where he was first introduced to the works of Socrates, Plato, and Aristotle.

After completing his Bachelor's degree, Caner pursued a Master's degree in History, which allowed him to delve deeper into the historical context and evolution of philosophical thought. He found the intersection of philosophy and history to be particularly fascinating, and it was during this time that his interest in Ancient Greek philosophy became a lifelong hobby.

In his free time, Caner enjoys exploring the writings and teachings of ancient philosophers, attending workshops and seminars, and engaging in online discussions with other enthusiasts. He is known for his analytical and critical thinking skills, as well as his ability to communicate complex ideas in a clear and concise manner.

Despite not pursuing philosophy as a profession, Caner's dedication to the subject has led him to become a respected voice in the community. He is passionate about sharing his knowledge and insights with others, and he hopes to inspire a new generation of thinkers to appreciate the rich and fascinating world of philosophy.